# 50 Keto Instant Pot Recipes for Home

By: Kelly Johnson

# Table of Contents

- Keto Instant Pot Chicken Curry
- Keto Instant Pot Beef Stew
- Keto Instant Pot Butter Chicken
- Keto Instant Pot Pork Carnitas
- Keto Instant Pot Beef Chili
- Keto Instant Pot Chicken Alfredo
- Keto Instant Pot Creamy Tuscan Chicken
- Keto Instant Pot Lemon Garlic Chicken
- Keto Instant Pot BBQ Pulled Pork
- Keto Instant Pot Beef and Broccoli
- Keto Instant Pot Buffalo Chicken Wings
- Keto Instant Pot Creamy Mushroom Soup
- Keto Instant Pot Pork Tenderloin with Garlic Herb Sauce
- Keto Instant Pot Chicken and Cauliflower Rice Soup
- Keto Instant Pot Beef Short Ribs
- Keto Instant Pot Cauliflower Mash
- Keto Instant Pot Taco Soup
- Keto Instant Pot Chicken Cacciatore
- Keto Instant Pot Garlic Parmesan Chicken Wings
- Keto Instant Pot Zucchini Noodles with Meatballs
- Keto Instant Pot Sausage and Kale Soup
- Keto Instant Pot Coconut Curry Shrimp
- Keto Instant Pot Creamy Garlic Tuscan Salmon
- Keto Instant Pot Spicy Beef Chili
- Keto Instant Pot Chicken Fajitas
- Keto Instant Pot Bacon and Cheese Egg Bites
- Keto Instant Pot Creamy Chicken and Spinach
- Keto Instant Pot Pork Ribs with Dry Rub
- Keto Instant Pot Cheesy Cauliflower Rice
- Keto Instant Pot Beef and Cabbage Soup
- Keto Instant Pot Creamy Garlic Parmesan Pork Chops
- Keto Instant Pot Chicken and Bacon Chowder
- Keto Instant Pot Italian Sausage and Peppers
- Keto Instant Pot Mississippi Pot Roast
- Keto Instant Pot Lemon Butter Salmon

- Keto Instant Pot Beef Stroganoff
- Keto Instant Pot Creamy Garlic Parmesan Chicken
- Keto Instant Pot Broccoli Cheese Soup
- Keto Instant Pot Pulled Chicken
- Keto Instant Pot Buffalo Chicken Dip
- Keto Instant Pot Mexican Shredded Chicken
- Keto Instant Pot Beef Brisket
- Keto Instant Pot Creamy Tuscan Pork Chops
- Keto Instant Pot Chicken Marsala
- Keto Instant Pot Ratatouille
- Keto Instant Pot Coconut Lime Chicken
- Keto Instant Pot Beef Bone Broth
- Keto Instant Pot Cauliflower Soup
- Keto Instant Pot Lemon Herb Chicken
- Keto Instant Pot Green Chile Pork Stew

**Keto Instant Pot Chicken Curry**

Ingredients:

- 1.5 lbs (680g) boneless, skinless chicken thighs, cut into bite-sized pieces
- 1 tablespoon coconut oil or ghee
- 1 onion, diced
- 3 cloves garlic, minced
- 1 tablespoon ginger, minced
- 1 tablespoon curry powder
- 1 teaspoon ground turmeric
- 1 teaspoon ground cumin
- 1 teaspoon ground coriander
- 1/2 teaspoon paprika
- 1/4 teaspoon cayenne pepper (adjust to taste)
- 1 cup chicken broth
- 1 can (14 oz) coconut milk
- Salt and pepper to taste
- Fresh cilantro, for garnish (optional)
- Cauliflower rice or zucchini noodles, for serving (optional)

Instructions:

1. Set your Instant Pot to sauté mode. Once hot, add the coconut oil or ghee.
2. Add the diced onion to the Instant Pot and sauté for 3-4 minutes, or until softened.
3. Add the minced garlic and ginger to the pot and sauté for another 1-2 minutes, until fragrant.
4. Add the curry powder, ground turmeric, ground cumin, ground coriander, paprika, and cayenne pepper to the pot. Stir well to coat the onions and spices.
5. Add the chicken pieces to the pot and sauté for 2-3 minutes, until lightly browned on all sides.
6. Pour in the chicken broth and deglaze the pot, scraping up any browned bits from the bottom.
7. Cancel the sauté mode and secure the lid on the Instant Pot. Set the Instant Pot to manual (pressure cook) mode and cook on high pressure for 8 minutes.

8. Once the cooking time is complete, allow the pressure to release naturally for 5 minutes, then carefully quick-release any remaining pressure.
9. Open the lid and stir in the coconut milk. Taste and adjust the seasoning with salt and pepper as needed.
10. Serve the Keto Instant Pot Chicken Curry hot, garnished with fresh cilantro if desired. Serve over cauliflower rice or zucchini noodles for a complete meal.

Enjoy your flavorful and satisfying Keto Instant Pot Chicken Curry!

**Keto Instant Pot Beef Stew**

- 1 turnip, peeled and diced (optional, for a low-carb option)
- 1 cup beef broth
- 1 tablespoon tomato paste
- 2 bay leaves
- 1 teaspoon dried thyme
- 1 teaspoon dried rosemary
- Salt and pepper to taste
- Chopped fresh parsley, for garnish (optional)

Instructions:

1. Set your Instant Pot to sauté mode. Once hot, add the olive oil.
2. Add the diced onion to the Instant Pot and sauté for 3-4 minutes, or until softened.
3. Add the minced garlic to the pot and sauté for another 1-2 minutes, until fragrant.
4. Add the beef stew meat to the pot and brown on all sides, about 5-7 minutes.
5. Stir in the diced carrots, celery, and turnip (if using) to the pot.
6. In a small bowl, mix together the beef broth and tomato paste until well combined. Pour the mixture into the Instant Pot.
7. Add the bay leaves, dried thyme, and dried rosemary to the pot. Season with salt and pepper to taste.
8. Cancel the sauté mode and secure the lid on the Instant Pot. Set the Instant Pot to manual (pressure cook) mode and cook on high pressure for 25 minutes.
9. Once the cooking time is complete, allow the pressure to release naturally for 10 minutes, then carefully quick-release any remaining pressure.
10. Open the lid and give the beef stew a stir. Taste and adjust the seasoning if needed.
11. Serve the Keto Instant Pot Beef Stew hot, garnished with chopped fresh parsley if desired.

Enjoy your delicious and hearty Keto Instant Pot Beef Stew!

**Keto Instant Pot Butter Chicken**

Ingredients:

- 1.5 lbs (about 680g) boneless, skinless chicken thighs, cut into bite-sized pieces
- 1 tablespoon ghee or butter
- 1 onion, finely chopped
- 3 cloves garlic, minced
- 1 tablespoon grated ginger
- 1 teaspoon ground turmeric
- 1 teaspoon ground cumin
- 1 teaspoon ground coriander
- 1 teaspoon paprika
- 1/2 teaspoon cayenne pepper (adjust to taste)
- 1/2 teaspoon ground cinnamon
- 1/2 teaspoon ground cloves
- 1/2 teaspoon ground cardamom
- 1 cup (240ml) tomato puree or crushed tomatoes
- 1/2 cup (120ml) heavy cream or coconut cream
- Salt and pepper, to taste
- Fresh cilantro, for garnish
- Cauliflower rice or low-carb naan, for serving (optional)

Instructions:

1. Set your Instant Pot to "Saute" mode and add the ghee or butter. Once melted, add the chopped onion and cook until softened, about 3-4 minutes.
2. Add the minced garlic and grated ginger, and cook for another minute until fragrant.
3. Add all the spices (turmeric, cumin, coriander, paprika, cayenne pepper, cinnamon, cloves, and cardamom) to the pot, stirring well to coat the onions and garlic.
4. Add the chicken pieces to the pot and cook until they are lightly browned on all sides, about 5 minutes.
5. Pour in the tomato puree or crushed tomatoes, stirring to combine with the chicken and spices.

6. Close the Instant Pot lid and set the valve to "Sealing." Cook on high pressure for 8 minutes.
7. Once the cooking time is complete, allow for a natural pressure release for 5 minutes, then carefully do a quick pressure release.
8. Stir in the heavy cream or coconut cream, and season with salt and pepper to taste. If the sauce is too thick, you can add a little water or broth to reach your desired consistency.
9. Serve the Keto Instant Pot Butter Chicken over cauliflower rice or with low-carb naan, garnished with fresh cilantro.

Enjoy your flavorful and keto-friendly Instant Pot Butter Chicken!

**Keto Instant Pot Pork Carnitas**

Ingredients:

- 2 lbs (about 900g) pork shoulder or pork butt, cut into large chunks
- 1 tablespoon olive oil
- 1 onion, diced
- 4 cloves garlic, minced
- 1 teaspoon ground cumin
- 1 teaspoon dried oregano
- 1 teaspoon smoked paprika
- 1 teaspoon chili powder
- 1 teaspoon salt
- 1/2 teaspoon black pepper
- 1/2 cup (120ml) chicken broth
- Juice of 2 limes
- Zest of 1 lime
- Fresh cilantro, chopped, for garnish
- Lime wedges, for serving
- Low-carb tortillas or lettuce leaves, for serving (optional)

Instructions:

1. Set your Instant Pot to "Saute" mode and add the olive oil. Once hot, add the diced onion and cook until softened, about 3-4 minutes.
2. Add the minced garlic to the pot and cook for another minute until fragrant.
3. Add the pork chunks to the pot and season with cumin, oregano, smoked paprika, chili powder, salt, and black pepper. Stir well to coat the pork evenly with the spices.
4. Pour in the chicken broth, lime juice, and lime zest, stirring to combine.
5. Close the Instant Pot lid and set the valve to "Sealing." Cook on high pressure for 40 minutes.
6. Once the cooking time is complete, allow for a natural pressure release for 10 minutes, then carefully do a quick pressure release.
7. Using a slotted spoon, transfer the pork chunks to a large baking sheet lined with parchment paper.
8. Preheat your oven's broiler on high heat.

9. Shred the pork using two forks and spread it out evenly on the baking sheet.
10. Place the baking sheet under the broiler for 5-7 minutes, or until the edges of the pork are crispy and browned.
11. Remove the pork from the oven and sprinkle with fresh chopped cilantro.
12. Serve the Keto Instant Pot Pork Carnitas with lime wedges and your choice of low-carb tortillas or lettuce leaves for wrapping, if desired.

Enjoy these flavorful and tender Keto Instant Pot Pork Carnitas for a delicious low-carb meal!

**Keto Instant Pot Beef Chili**

Ingredients:

- 2 lbs (about 900g) ground beef
- 1 tablespoon olive oil
- 1 onion, diced
- 3 cloves garlic, minced
- 1 bell pepper, diced (any color)
- 1 can (14.5 oz) diced tomatoes, undrained
- 1 can (6 oz) tomato paste
- 1 cup (240ml) beef broth
- 2 tablespoons chili powder
- 1 tablespoon ground cumin
- 1 teaspoon smoked paprika
- 1 teaspoon dried oregano
- 1/2 teaspoon cayenne pepper (adjust to taste)
- Salt and black pepper, to taste
- Optional toppings: shredded cheddar cheese, sour cream, diced avocado, chopped cilantro

Instructions:

1. Set your Instant Pot to "Saute" mode and add the olive oil. Once hot, add the diced onion and bell pepper. Cook until softened, about 3-4 minutes.
2. Add the minced garlic and cook for another minute until fragrant.
3. Add the ground beef to the pot and cook until browned, breaking it apart with a spoon as it cooks.
4. Once the beef is browned, add the diced tomatoes, tomato paste, beef broth, chili powder, cumin, smoked paprika, oregano, and cayenne pepper to the pot. Stir well to combine.
5. Close the Instant Pot lid and set the valve to "Sealing." Cook on high pressure for 15 minutes.
6. Once the cooking time is complete, allow for a natural pressure release for 10 minutes, then carefully do a quick pressure release.
7. Open the Instant Pot lid and stir the chili. Taste and adjust seasoning with salt and black pepper if needed.

8. Serve the Keto Instant Pot Beef Chili hot, garnished with your favorite toppings such as shredded cheddar cheese, sour cream, diced avocado, and chopped cilantro.

Enjoy this hearty and flavorful Keto Instant Pot Beef Chili for a satisfying low-carb meal!

**Keto Instant Pot Chicken Alfredo**

Ingredients:

- 1.5 lbs (about 680g) boneless, skinless chicken breasts, cut into bite-sized pieces
- 2 tablespoons butter
- 3 cloves garlic, minced
- 1 cup (240ml) chicken broth
- 1 cup (240ml) heavy cream
- 1/2 cup (50g) grated Parmesan cheese
- 1/2 teaspoon garlic powder
- 1/2 teaspoon onion powder
- 1/2 teaspoon Italian seasoning
- Salt and black pepper, to taste
- Fresh parsley, chopped, for garnish
- Low-carb pasta or zucchini noodles, for serving (optional)

Instructions:

1. Set your Instant Pot to "Saute" mode and add the butter. Once melted, add the minced garlic and cook for about 1 minute until fragrant.
2. Add the chicken pieces to the pot and cook until they are lightly browned on all sides, about 5 minutes.
3. Pour in the chicken broth and deglaze the bottom of the pot, scraping up any browned bits.
4. Add the heavy cream, grated Parmesan cheese, garlic powder, onion powder, and Italian seasoning to the pot. Stir well to combine.
5. Close the Instant Pot lid and set the valve to "Sealing." Cook on high pressure for 8 minutes.
6. Once the cooking time is complete, allow for a natural pressure release for 5 minutes, then carefully do a quick pressure release.
7. Open the Instant Pot lid and stir the chicken Alfredo sauce. Taste and adjust seasoning with salt and black pepper if needed.
8. Serve the Keto Instant Pot Chicken Alfredo hot, garnished with chopped fresh parsley. You can serve it over low-carb pasta or zucchini noodles if desired.

Enjoy this creamy and indulgent Keto Instant Pot Chicken Alfredo for a satisfying low-carb meal!

**Keto Instant Pot Creamy Tuscan Chicken**

Ingredients:

- 1.5 lbs (about 680g) boneless, skinless chicken breasts, cut into bite-sized pieces
- 2 tablespoons olive oil
- 3 cloves garlic, minced
- 1 small onion, finely chopped
- 1 cup (240ml) chicken broth
- 1 cup (240ml) heavy cream
- 1/2 cup (50g) grated Parmesan cheese
- 1/2 cup (120g) sun-dried tomatoes, chopped
- 1/2 cup (75g) baby spinach leaves
- 1 teaspoon dried thyme
- Salt and black pepper, to taste
- Fresh basil leaves, chopped, for garnish

Instructions:

1. Set your Instant Pot to "Saute" mode and add the olive oil. Once hot, add the minced garlic and chopped onion. Cook until softened, about 3-4 minutes.
2. Add the chicken pieces to the pot and cook until they are lightly browned on all sides, about 5 minutes.
3. Pour in the chicken broth, heavy cream, grated Parmesan cheese, chopped sun-dried tomatoes, and dried thyme. Stir well to combine.
4. Close the Instant Pot lid and set the valve to "Sealing." Cook on high pressure for 8 minutes.
5. Once the cooking time is complete, allow for a natural pressure release for 5 minutes, then carefully do a quick pressure release.
6. Open the Instant Pot lid and stir the creamy Tuscan chicken mixture. Taste and adjust seasoning with salt and black pepper if needed.
7. Stir in the baby spinach leaves and let them wilt slightly in the hot mixture.
8. Serve the Keto Instant Pot Creamy Tuscan Chicken hot, garnished with chopped fresh basil leaves.

Enjoy this rich and flavorful Keto Instant Pot Creamy Tuscan Chicken for a comforting low-carb meal!

**Keto Instant Pot Lemon Garlic Chicken**

Ingredients:

- 1.5 lbs (about 680g) boneless, skinless chicken breasts
- 2 tablespoons olive oil
- 4 cloves garlic, minced
- Zest of 1 lemon
- Juice of 1 lemon
- 1 cup (240ml) chicken broth
- 1 teaspoon dried thyme
- 1 teaspoon dried rosemary
- Salt and black pepper, to taste
- Fresh parsley, chopped, for garnish

Instructions:

1. Set your Instant Pot to "Saute" mode and add the olive oil. Once hot, add the minced garlic and cook for about 1 minute until fragrant.
2. Add the chicken breasts to the pot and cook until they are lightly browned on both sides, about 3-4 minutes per side.
3. In a small bowl, combine the lemon zest, lemon juice, chicken broth, dried thyme, and dried rosemary.
4. Pour the lemon herb mixture over the chicken in the Instant Pot.
5. Close the Instant Pot lid and set the valve to "Sealing." Cook on high pressure for 10 minutes.
6. Once the cooking time is complete, allow for a natural pressure release for 5 minutes, then carefully do a quick pressure release.
7. Open the Instant Pot lid and transfer the chicken breasts to a serving plate.
8. If desired, you can thicken the sauce by setting the Instant Pot to "Saute" mode again and simmering the sauce for a few minutes until it reaches your desired consistency.
9. Season the sauce with salt and black pepper to taste.
10. Serve the Keto Instant Pot Lemon Garlic Chicken hot, garnished with chopped fresh parsley.

Enjoy this bright and flavorful Keto Instant Pot Lemon Garlic Chicken for a refreshing low-carb meal!

**Keto Instant Pot BBQ Pulled Pork**

Ingredients:

- 3 lbs (about 1.4 kg) pork shoulder or pork butt, cut into large chunks
- 1 tablespoon olive oil
- 1 cup (240ml) sugar-free BBQ sauce
- 1/2 cup (120ml) chicken broth
- 1/4 cup (60ml) apple cider vinegar
- 2 tablespoons Worcestershire sauce (ensure it's low-carb)
- 1 tablespoon smoked paprika
- 1 tablespoon garlic powder
- 1 tablespoon onion powder
- 1 teaspoon ground mustard
- 1 teaspoon chili powder
- Salt and black pepper, to taste
- Low-carb sandwich buns or lettuce leaves, for serving (optional)
- Coleslaw, for topping (optional)

Instructions:

1. Set your Instant Pot to "Saute" mode and add the olive oil. Once hot, add the pork chunks and brown them on all sides, about 3-4 minutes per side.
2. In a mixing bowl, combine the sugar-free BBQ sauce, chicken broth, apple cider vinegar, Worcestershire sauce, smoked paprika, garlic powder, onion powder, ground mustard, and chili powder. Mix well.
3. Pour the BBQ sauce mixture over the pork in the Instant Pot.
4. Close the Instant Pot lid and set the valve to "Sealing." Cook on high pressure for 60 minutes.
5. Once the cooking time is complete, allow for a natural pressure release for 10 minutes, then carefully do a quick pressure release.
6. Open the Instant Pot lid and transfer the pork chunks to a cutting board. Shred the pork using two forks.
7. If desired, set the Instant Pot to "Saute" mode again and simmer the sauce for a few minutes to thicken it.
8. Return the shredded pork to the Instant Pot and stir to coat it in the BBQ sauce.
9. Season with salt and black pepper to taste.

10. Serve the Keto Instant Pot BBQ Pulled Pork hot, piled onto low-carb sandwich buns or lettuce leaves, and topped with coleslaw if desired.

Enjoy this savory and satisfying Keto Instant Pot BBQ Pulled Pork for a delicious low-carb meal!

## Keto Instant Pot Beef and Broccoli

Ingredients:

- 1.5 lbs (about 680g) flank steak, thinly sliced against the grain
- 1/2 cup (120ml) soy sauce or tamari sauce (for gluten-free option)
- 1/4 cup (60ml) beef broth
- 2 tablespoons olive oil
- 4 cloves garlic, minced
- 1 teaspoon grated ginger
- 1 tablespoon erythritol or low-carb sweetener of choice
- 1 tablespoon sesame oil
- 2 cups (300g) broccoli florets
- 1 tablespoon cornstarch or arrowroot powder (optional, for thickening)
- Sesame seeds, for garnish
- Sliced green onions, for garnish
- Cauliflower rice or shirataki noodles, for serving (optional)

Instructions:

1. In a bowl, combine the soy sauce (or tamari sauce), beef broth, olive oil, minced garlic, grated ginger, erythritol, and sesame oil. Mix well.
2. Place the thinly sliced flank steak in the Instant Pot and pour the sauce mixture over it. Toss to coat the meat evenly.
3. Close the Instant Pot lid and set the valve to "Sealing." Cook on high pressure for 8 minutes.
4. Once the cooking time is complete, perform a quick pressure release.
5. Open the Instant Pot lid and add the broccoli florets to the pot. Stir to combine with the beef and sauce.
6. If you prefer a thicker sauce, mix the cornstarch or arrowroot powder with a little water to form a slurry. Stir the slurry into the beef and broccoli mixture.
7. Set the Instant Pot to "Saute" mode and cook for an additional 2-3 minutes, or until the sauce has thickened and the broccoli is tender-crisp.
8. Serve the Keto Instant Pot Beef and Broccoli hot, garnished with sesame seeds and sliced green onions. Optionally, serve over cauliflower rice or shirataki noodles.

Enjoy this flavorful and satisfying Keto Instant Pot Beef and Broccoli for a delicious low-carb meal!

**Keto Instant Pot Buffalo Chicken Wings**

Ingredients:

- 2 lbs (about 900g) chicken wings
- 1/2 cup (120ml) hot sauce (check for low-carb options)
- 1/4 cup (60g) unsalted butter
- 2 cloves garlic, minced
- 1 teaspoon Worcestershire sauce (optional, ensure it's low-carb)
- Salt and black pepper, to taste
- Ranch or blue cheese dressing, for serving
- Celery sticks, for serving

Instructions:

1. Place a trivet in the bottom of the Instant Pot insert and add 1 cup of water.
2. Season the chicken wings with salt and black pepper.
3. In a small saucepan over medium heat, melt the butter. Once melted, add the minced garlic and cook for about 1 minute until fragrant.
4. Stir in the hot sauce and Worcestershire sauce (if using). Remove from heat.
5. In a large mixing bowl, toss the chicken wings with half of the buffalo sauce until well coated.
6. Arrange the chicken wings on the trivet in the Instant Pot.
7. Close the Instant Pot lid and set the valve to "Sealing." Cook on high pressure for 10 minutes.
8. Once the cooking time is complete, perform a quick pressure release.
9. Preheat the oven broiler on high heat.
10. Carefully transfer the cooked chicken wings to a baking sheet lined with aluminum foil.
11. Brush the wings with the remaining buffalo sauce.
12. Place the baking sheet under the broiler for 3-5 minutes, or until the wings are golden brown and crispy.
13. Serve the Keto Instant Pot Buffalo Chicken Wings hot, with ranch or blue cheese dressing and celery sticks on the side for dipping.

Enjoy these spicy and flavorful Keto Instant Pot Buffalo Chicken Wings for a delicious low-carb snack or meal!

**Keto Instant Pot Creamy Mushroom Soup**

Ingredients:

- 1 lb (about 450g) cremini mushrooms, sliced
- 1 small onion, diced
- 2 cloves garlic, minced
- 2 tablespoons butter
- 4 cups (960ml) chicken or vegetable broth
- 1 cup (240ml) heavy cream
- 2 tablespoons cream cheese
- 1 teaspoon dried thyme
- Salt and black pepper, to taste
- Fresh parsley, chopped, for garnish

Instructions:

1. Set your Instant Pot to "Saute" mode and melt the butter.
2. Add the diced onion and minced garlic to the pot. Cook until the onion is translucent, about 3-4 minutes.
3. Add the sliced mushrooms to the pot and cook until they release their moisture and begin to brown, about 5-7 minutes.
4. Pour in the chicken or vegetable broth and add the dried thyme. Stir to combine.
5. Close the Instant Pot lid and set the valve to "Sealing." Cook on high pressure for 5 minutes.
6. Once the cooking time is complete, perform a quick pressure release.
7. Open the Instant Pot lid and stir in the heavy cream and cream cheese until the cream cheese is melted and the soup is creamy.
8. Season the soup with salt and black pepper to taste.
9. If desired, use an immersion blender to blend some of the soup to reach your desired consistency. Alternatively, you can transfer a portion of the soup to a blender and blend until smooth, then return it to the pot.
10. Serve the Keto Instant Pot Creamy Mushroom Soup hot, garnished with chopped fresh parsley.

Enjoy this rich and flavorful Keto Instant Pot Creamy Mushroom Soup for a comforting low-carb meal!

**Keto Instant Pot Pork Tenderloin with Garlic Herb Sauce**

Ingredients:

- 2 lbs (about 900g) pork tenderloin
- 2 tablespoons olive oil
- Salt and black pepper, to taste
- 4 cloves garlic, minced
- 1 teaspoon dried thyme
- 1 teaspoon dried rosemary
- 1/2 cup (120ml) chicken or vegetable broth
- 1/4 cup (60ml) heavy cream
- 2 tablespoons cream cheese
- 1 tablespoon Dijon mustard
- Fresh parsley, chopped, for garnish

Instructions:

1. Season the pork tenderloin generously with salt and black pepper.
2. Set your Instant Pot to "Saute" mode and add the olive oil. Once hot, add the seasoned pork tenderloin and sear on all sides until browned, about 2-3 minutes per side. Remove the pork from the Instant Pot and set aside.
3. Add the minced garlic, dried thyme, and dried rosemary to the pot. Cook for about 1 minute until fragrant.
4. Pour in the chicken or vegetable broth, scraping up any browned bits from the bottom of the pot.
5. Return the seared pork tenderloin to the Instant Pot.
6. Close the Instant Pot lid and set the valve to "Sealing." Cook on high pressure for 8 minutes.
7. Once the cooking time is complete, allow for a natural pressure release for 5 minutes, then carefully do a quick pressure release.
8. Open the Instant Pot lid and transfer the pork tenderloin to a serving platter. Cover with foil to keep warm.
9. Set the Instant Pot to "Saute" mode again. Stir in the heavy cream, cream cheese, and Dijon mustard until the sauce is smooth and creamy. Let it simmer for a few minutes until slightly thickened.
10. Taste the sauce and adjust seasoning with salt and black pepper if needed.

11. Slice the pork tenderloin and serve it hot, drizzled with the creamy garlic herb sauce. Garnish with chopped fresh parsley.

Enjoy this succulent and flavorful Keto Instant Pot Pork Tenderloin with Garlic Herb Sauce for a delicious low-carb meal!

**Keto Instant Pot Chicken and Cauliflower Rice Soup**

Ingredients:

- 1 lb (about 450g) boneless, skinless chicken breasts, cut into bite-sized pieces
- 2 tablespoons olive oil
- 1 onion, diced
- 2 carrots, diced
- 2 celery stalks, diced
- 3 cloves garlic, minced
- 4 cups (960ml) chicken broth
- 1 head cauliflower, riced (about 4 cups)
- 1 teaspoon dried thyme
- 1 teaspoon dried rosemary
- Salt and black pepper, to taste
- Fresh parsley, chopped, for garnish

Instructions:

1. Set your Instant Pot to "Saute" mode and add the olive oil. Once hot, add the diced onion, carrots, and celery. Cook until softened, about 3-4 minutes.
2. Add the minced garlic to the pot and cook for another minute until fragrant.
3. Add the chicken pieces to the pot and cook until they are lightly browned on all sides, about 5 minutes.
4. Pour in the chicken broth, dried thyme, and dried rosemary. Stir to combine.
5. Close the Instant Pot lid and set the valve to "Sealing." Cook on high pressure for 8 minutes.
6. Once the cooking time is complete, perform a quick pressure release.
7. Open the Instant Pot lid and stir in the riced cauliflower. The residual heat will cook the cauliflower without needing to pressure cook it.
8. Season the soup with salt and black pepper to taste.
9. If desired, use an immersion blender to blend some of the soup to reach your desired consistency.
10. Serve the Keto Instant Pot Chicken and Cauliflower Rice Soup hot, garnished with chopped fresh parsley.

Enjoy this hearty and nutritious Keto Instant Pot Chicken and Cauliflower Rice Soup for a satisfying low-carb meal!

**Keto Instant Pot Beef Short Ribs**

Ingredients:

- 4 lbs (about 1.8 kg) beef short ribs
- Salt and black pepper, to taste
- 2 tablespoons olive oil
- 1 onion, diced
- 2 carrots, diced
- 2 celery stalks, diced
- 4 cloves garlic, minced
- 2 cups (480ml) beef broth
- 1 cup (240ml) dry red wine (optional, omit for strict keto)
- 2 tablespoons tomato paste
- 2 tablespoons Worcestershire sauce (ensure it's low-carb)
- 1 teaspoon dried thyme
- 1 teaspoon dried rosemary
- 2 bay leaves
- Fresh parsley, chopped, for garnish

Instructions:

1. Season the beef short ribs generously with salt and black pepper.
2. Set your Instant Pot to "Saute" mode and add the olive oil. Once hot, add the beef short ribs and sear on all sides until browned, about 3-4 minutes per side. Remove the short ribs from the Instant Pot and set aside.
3. Add the diced onion, carrots, and celery to the pot. Cook until softened, about 3-4 minutes.
4. Add the minced garlic to the pot and cook for another minute until fragrant.
5. Pour in the beef broth and red wine (if using), scraping up any browned bits from the bottom of the pot.
6. Stir in the tomato paste, Worcestershire sauce, dried thyme, dried rosemary, and bay leaves.
7. Return the seared beef short ribs to the Instant Pot, nestling them into the liquid and vegetables.
8. Close the Instant Pot lid and set the valve to "Sealing." Cook on high pressure for 45 minutes.

9. Once the cooking time is complete, allow for a natural pressure release for 10 minutes, then carefully do a quick pressure release.
10. Open the Instant Pot lid and transfer the beef short ribs to a serving platter. Cover with foil to keep warm.
11. If desired, set the Instant Pot to "Saute" mode again and simmer the sauce for a few minutes to thicken it.
12. Serve the Keto Instant Pot Beef Short Ribs hot, garnished with chopped fresh parsley.

Enjoy these tender and flavorful Keto Instant Pot Beef Short Ribs for a satisfying low-carb meal!

**Keto Instant Pot Cauliflower Mash**

Ingredients:

- 1 large head of cauliflower, cut into florets
- 2 cloves garlic, minced
- 2 tablespoons butter
- 1/4 cup (60ml) heavy cream
- 1/4 cup (25g) grated Parmesan cheese
- Salt and black pepper, to taste
- Chopped chives or parsley, for garnish (optional)

Instructions:

1. Place the cauliflower florets and minced garlic in the Instant Pot insert.
2. Add water to the Instant Pot until it reaches just below the level of the cauliflower.
3. Close the Instant Pot lid and set the valve to "Sealing." Cook on high pressure for 4 minutes.
4. Once the cooking time is complete, perform a quick pressure release.
5. Open the Instant Pot lid and drain the cauliflower well.
6. Return the cauliflower and garlic to the Instant Pot.
7. Add the butter, heavy cream, and grated Parmesan cheese to the pot.
8. Use an immersion blender to blend the cauliflower until smooth and creamy. Alternatively, you can transfer the cauliflower to a food processor or blender to puree.
9. Season the cauliflower mash with salt and black pepper to taste.
10. Serve the Keto Instant Pot Cauliflower Mash hot, garnished with chopped chives or parsley if desired.

Enjoy this velvety and satisfying Keto Instant Pot Cauliflower Mash as a delicious low-carb side dish!

**Keto Instant Pot Taco Soup**

Ingredients:

- 1 lb (about 450g) ground beef or turkey
- 1 tablespoon olive oil
- 1 small onion, diced
- 2 cloves garlic, minced
- 1 bell pepper, diced
- 1 can (14.5 oz) diced tomatoes, undrained
- 1 can (4 oz) diced green chilies
- 2 cups (480ml) beef or chicken broth
- 1 tablespoon chili powder
- 1 teaspoon ground cumin
- 1 teaspoon paprika
- 1/2 teaspoon dried oregano
- Salt and black pepper, to taste
- Optional toppings: shredded cheddar cheese, sour cream, sliced avocado, chopped cilantro, lime wedges

Instructions:

1. Set your Instant Pot to "Saute" mode and add the olive oil. Once hot, add the diced onion and bell pepper. Cook until softened, about 3-4 minutes.
2. Add the minced garlic to the pot and cook for another minute until fragrant.
3. Add the ground beef or turkey to the pot and cook until browned, breaking it apart with a spoon as it cooks.
4. Once the meat is browned, add the diced tomatoes, diced green chilies, beef or chicken broth, chili powder, ground cumin, paprika, dried oregano, salt, and black pepper to the pot. Stir well to combine.
5. Close the Instant Pot lid and set the valve to "Sealing." Cook on high pressure for 8 minutes.
6. Once the cooking time is complete, allow for a natural pressure release for 5 minutes, then carefully do a quick pressure release.
7. Open the Instant Pot lid and stir the taco soup.
8. Serve the Keto Instant Pot Taco Soup hot, topped with your favorite toppings such as shredded cheddar cheese, sour cream, sliced avocado, chopped cilantro, and lime wedges.

Enjoy this hearty and flavorful Keto Instant Pot Taco Soup for a delicious low-carb meal!

**Keto Instant Pot Chicken Cacciatore**

Ingredients:

- 2 lbs (about 900g) bone-in, skin-on chicken thighs or drumsticks
- Salt and black pepper, to taste
- 2 tablespoons olive oil
- 1 onion, diced
- 2 bell peppers, sliced
- 3 cloves garlic, minced
- 1 can (14.5 oz) diced tomatoes, undrained
- 1 can (6 oz) tomato paste
- 1/2 cup (120ml) chicken broth
- 1 teaspoon dried oregano
- 1 teaspoon dried basil
- 1/2 teaspoon dried thyme
- 1/2 teaspoon dried rosemary
- 1/2 teaspoon red pepper flakes (optional)
- 1/2 cup (75g) sliced black olives (optional)
- Fresh parsley, chopped, for garnish

Instructions:

1. Season the chicken thighs or drumsticks with salt and black pepper.
2. Set your Instant Pot to "Saute" mode and add the olive oil. Once hot, add the chicken pieces and brown them on all sides, about 3-4 minutes per side. Remove the chicken from the Instant Pot and set aside.
3. Add the diced onion and sliced bell peppers to the pot. Cook until softened, about 3-4 minutes.
4. Add the minced garlic to the pot and cook for another minute until fragrant.
5. Stir in the diced tomatoes, tomato paste, chicken broth, dried oregano, dried basil, dried thyme, dried rosemary, and red pepper flakes (if using). Mix well.
6. Return the browned chicken pieces to the Instant Pot, nestling them into the sauce.
7. Close the Instant Pot lid and set the valve to "Sealing." Cook on high pressure for 10 minutes.

8. Once the cooking time is complete, allow for a natural pressure release for 10 minutes, then carefully do a quick pressure release.
9. Open the Instant Pot lid and stir in the sliced black olives (if using).
10. Serve the Keto Instant Pot Chicken Cacciatore hot, garnished with chopped fresh parsley.

Enjoy this flavorful and comforting Keto Instant Pot Chicken Cacciatore for a delicious low-carb meal!

## Keto Instant Pot Garlic Parmesan Chicken Wings

Ingredients:

- 2 lbs (about 900g) chicken wings
- Salt and black pepper, to taste
- 2 tablespoons olive oil
- 4 cloves garlic, minced
- 1/4 cup (60g) unsalted butter
- 1/4 cup (25g) grated Parmesan cheese
- 1 tablespoon dried parsley
- 1/2 teaspoon dried thyme
- 1/2 teaspoon dried rosemary
- 1/2 teaspoon dried oregano
- Pinch of red pepper flakes (optional)
- Fresh parsley, chopped, for garnish

Instructions:

1. Season the chicken wings with salt and black pepper.
2. Set your Instant Pot to "Saute" mode and add the olive oil. Once hot, add the chicken wings and brown them on all sides, about 3-4 minutes per side. You may need to do this in batches depending on the size of your Instant Pot.
3. Once the chicken wings are browned, transfer them to a plate and set aside.
4. In the same Instant Pot, add the minced garlic and cook for about 1 minute until fragrant.
5. Add the butter to the pot and let it melt.
6. Stir in the grated Parmesan cheese, dried parsley, dried thyme, dried rosemary, dried oregano, and red pepper flakes (if using). Mix well to combine.
7. Return the chicken wings to the Instant Pot, coating them in the garlic Parmesan butter mixture.
8. Close the Instant Pot lid and set the valve to "Sealing." Cook on high pressure for 5 minutes.
9. Once the cooking time is complete, allow for a natural pressure release for 5 minutes, then carefully do a quick pressure release.
10. Open the Instant Pot lid and transfer the chicken wings to a serving plate.

11. If desired, set the Instant Pot to "Saute" mode again and simmer the sauce for a few minutes to thicken it.
12. Pour the garlic Parmesan sauce over the chicken wings.
13. Serve the Keto Instant Pot Garlic Parmesan Chicken Wings hot, garnished with chopped fresh parsley.

Enjoy these crispy and flavorful Keto Instant Pot Garlic Parmesan Chicken Wings for a delicious low-carb appetizer or meal!

**Keto Instant Pot Zucchini Noodles with Meatballs**

Ingredients:

For the meatballs:

- 1 lb (about 450g) ground beef or turkey
- 1/4 cup (25g) grated Parmesan cheese
- 1/4 cup (30g) almond flour
- 1 egg
- 2 cloves garlic, minced
- 1 teaspoon dried oregano
- 1 teaspoon dried basil
- Salt and black pepper, to taste
- Olive oil, for cooking

For the zucchini noodles:

- 4 medium zucchinis, spiralized into noodles
- 2 tablespoons olive oil
- 3 cloves garlic, minced
- 1/4 teaspoon red pepper flakes (optional)
- Salt and black pepper, to taste
- Fresh basil, chopped, for garnish

Instructions:

1. In a large bowl, combine the ground meat, grated Parmesan cheese, almond flour, egg, minced garlic, dried oregano, dried basil, salt, and black pepper. Mix well until all ingredients are evenly combined.
2. Form the mixture into meatballs, about 1 inch in diameter.
3. Set your Instant Pot to "Saute" mode and add a bit of olive oil. Once hot, add the meatballs and cook until browned on all sides, about 3-4 minutes. You may need to do this in batches depending on the size of your Instant Pot. Remove the meatballs and set aside.

4. In the same Instant Pot, add a bit more olive oil if needed. Add the minced garlic and red pepper flakes (if using). Cook for about 1 minute until fragrant.
5. Add the spiralized zucchini noodles to the pot. Cook for about 2-3 minutes until slightly softened.
6. Return the meatballs to the Instant Pot, nestling them among the zucchini noodles.
7. Close the Instant Pot lid and set the valve to "Sealing." Cook on high pressure for 1 minute.
8. Once the cooking time is complete, perform a quick pressure release.
9. Open the Instant Pot lid and gently toss the zucchini noodles and meatballs together.
10. Season with salt and black pepper to taste.
11. Serve the Keto Instant Pot Zucchini Noodles with Meatballs hot, garnished with chopped fresh basil.

Enjoy this delicious and healthy Keto Instant Pot meal!

**Keto Instant Pot Sausage and Kale Soup**

Ingredients:

- 1 lb (about 450g) Italian sausage, casings removed
- 1 tablespoon olive oil
- 1 onion, diced
- 3 cloves garlic, minced
- 4 cups (960ml) chicken broth
- 1 can (14.5 oz) diced tomatoes, undrained
- 1 bunch kale, stems removed and leaves chopped
- 1 teaspoon dried oregano
- 1/2 teaspoon dried thyme
- 1/2 teaspoon dried rosemary
- Salt and black pepper, to taste
- Grated Parmesan cheese, for garnish (optional)

Instructions:

1. Set your Instant Pot to "Saute" mode and add the olive oil. Once hot, add the Italian sausage, breaking it apart with a spoon as it cooks. Cook until browned and no longer pink, about 5-7 minutes.
2. Add the diced onion to the pot and cook until softened, about 3-4 minutes.
3. Add the minced garlic to the pot and cook for another minute until fragrant.
4. Pour in the chicken broth and diced tomatoes (with their juices) to the pot. Stir well to combine.
5. Add the chopped kale leaves, dried oregano, dried thyme, and dried rosemary to the pot. Mix well.
6. Close the Instant Pot lid and set the valve to "Sealing." Cook on high pressure for 5 minutes.
7. Once the cooking time is complete, allow for a natural pressure release for 5 minutes, then carefully do a quick pressure release.
8. Open the Instant Pot lid and stir the soup. Season with salt and black pepper to taste.
9. Serve the Keto Instant Pot Sausage and Kale Soup hot, garnished with grated Parmesan cheese if desired.

Enjoy this comforting and nutritious Keto Instant Pot soup!

**Keto Instant Pot Coconut Curry Shrimp**

Ingredients:

- 1 lb (about 450g) large shrimp, peeled and deveined
- 2 tablespoons coconut oil
- 1 onion, diced
- 3 cloves garlic, minced
- 1 bell pepper, diced
- 1 zucchini, diced
- 1 tablespoon curry powder
- 1 teaspoon ground turmeric
- 1 teaspoon ground cumin
- 1 teaspoon ground coriander
- 1/2 teaspoon ground ginger
- 1/4 teaspoon red pepper flakes (optional)
- 1 can (14 oz) coconut milk
- 1 tablespoon fish sauce (optional)
- Salt and black pepper, to taste
- Fresh cilantro, chopped, for garnish
- Lime wedges, for serving

Instructions:

1. Set your Instant Pot to "Saute" mode and add the coconut oil. Once hot, add the diced onion, minced garlic, diced bell pepper, and diced zucchini. Cook until softened, about 3-4 minutes.
2. Stir in the curry powder, ground turmeric, ground cumin, ground coriander, ground ginger, and red pepper flakes (if using). Cook for another minute until fragrant.
3. Pour in the coconut milk and fish sauce (if using). Stir well to combine.
4. Add the peeled and deveined shrimp to the Instant Pot, stirring to coat them in the coconut curry mixture.
5. Close the Instant Pot lid and set the valve to "Sealing." Cook on high pressure for 1 minute.
6. Once the cooking time is complete, perform a quick pressure release.
7. Open the Instant Pot lid and season the coconut curry shrimp with salt and black pepper to taste.

8. Serve the Keto Instant Pot Coconut Curry Shrimp hot, garnished with chopped fresh cilantro and lime wedges on the side.

Enjoy this fragrant and flavorful Keto Instant Pot Coconut Curry Shrimp for a delicious low-carb meal!

**Keto Instant Pot Creamy Garlic Tuscan Salmon**

Ingredients:

- 4 salmon fillets (about 6 oz each)
- Salt and black pepper, to taste
- 2 tablespoons olive oil
- 4 cloves garlic, minced
- 1/2 cup (120ml) chicken or vegetable broth
- 1 cup (240ml) heavy cream
- 1/4 cup (25g) grated Parmesan cheese
- 1/4 cup (60g) sun-dried tomatoes, chopped
- 1 cup (30g) fresh spinach leaves
- 1 teaspoon dried thyme
- 1 teaspoon dried rosemary
- Salt and black pepper, to taste
- Fresh parsley, chopped, for garnish
- Lemon wedges, for serving

Instructions:

1. Season the salmon fillets with salt and black pepper.
2. Set your Instant Pot to "Saute" mode and add the olive oil. Once hot, add the minced garlic and cook for about 1 minute until fragrant.
3. Pour in the chicken or vegetable broth and stir to deglaze the bottom of the pot.
4. Add the heavy cream, grated Parmesan cheese, chopped sun-dried tomatoes, fresh spinach leaves, dried thyme, and dried rosemary to the pot. Mix well.
5. Nestle the seasoned salmon fillets into the creamy garlic Tuscan sauce in the Instant Pot.
6. Close the Instant Pot lid and set the valve to "Sealing." Cook on high pressure for 3 minutes.
7. Once the cooking time is complete, perform a quick pressure release.
8. Open the Instant Pot lid and carefully remove the salmon fillets to a serving plate.
9. Stir the creamy sauce in the Instant Pot until well combined. Taste and adjust seasoning with salt and black pepper if needed.

10. Serve the Keto Instant Pot Creamy Garlic Tuscan Salmon hot, spooning the sauce over the salmon fillets. Garnish with chopped fresh parsley and serve with lemon wedges on the side.

Enjoy this rich and flavorful Keto Instant Pot Creamy Garlic Tuscan Salmon for a delicious low-carb meal!

**Keto Instant Pot Spicy Beef Chili**

Ingredients:

- 2 lbs (about 900g) ground beef
- 1 tablespoon olive oil
- 1 onion, diced
- 3 cloves garlic, minced
- 1 bell pepper, diced
- 2 jalapeño peppers, diced (remove seeds for less heat)
- 2 tablespoons tomato paste
- 2 cans (14.5 oz each) diced tomatoes, undrained
- 1 can (6 oz) tomato paste
- 2 cups (480ml) beef broth
- 2 tablespoons chili powder
- 1 tablespoon ground cumin
- 1 teaspoon paprika
- 1/2 teaspoon cayenne pepper (adjust to taste)
- Salt and black pepper, to taste
- Optional toppings: shredded cheddar cheese, sour cream, sliced green onions, chopped cilantro, avocado slices

Instructions:

1. Set your Instant Pot to "Saute" mode and add the olive oil. Once hot, add the ground beef and cook until browned, breaking it apart with a spoon as it cooks.
2. Add the diced onion, minced garlic, diced bell pepper, and diced jalapeño peppers to the pot. Cook until the vegetables are softened, about 3-4 minutes.
3. Stir in the tomato paste, diced tomatoes (with their juices), beef broth, chili powder, ground cumin, paprika, cayenne pepper, salt, and black pepper.
4. Close the Instant Pot lid and set the valve to "Sealing." Cook on high pressure for 10 minutes.
5. Once the cooking time is complete, allow for a natural pressure release for 10 minutes, then carefully do a quick pressure release.
6. Open the Instant Pot lid and stir the chili. Taste and adjust seasoning if needed.
7. Serve the Keto Instant Pot Spicy Beef Chili hot, garnished with your favorite toppings such as shredded cheddar cheese, sour cream, sliced green onions, chopped cilantro, and avocado slices.

Enjoy this hearty and flavorful Keto Instant Pot Spicy Beef Chili for a satisfying low-carb meal!

**Keto Instant Pot Chicken Fajitas**

Ingredients:

- 1.5 lbs (about 680g) boneless, skinless chicken breasts, sliced into strips
- 2 tablespoons olive oil
- 1 onion, sliced
- 1 bell pepper, sliced
- 1 jalapeño pepper, sliced (optional)
- 3 cloves garlic, minced
- 1 tablespoon chili powder
- 1 teaspoon ground cumin
- 1 teaspoon paprika
- 1/2 teaspoon dried oregano
- Salt and black pepper, to taste
- Juice of 1 lime
- 1/4 cup (60ml) chicken broth
- Optional toppings: shredded cheese, sour cream, guacamole, salsa, chopped cilantro, lime wedges
- Low-carb tortillas or lettuce wraps, for serving (optional)

Instructions:

1. Set your Instant Pot to "Saute" mode and add the olive oil. Once hot, add the sliced chicken breasts and cook until browned, about 3-4 minutes.
2. Add the sliced onion, sliced bell pepper, sliced jalapeño pepper (if using), and minced garlic to the pot. Cook until the vegetables are softened, about 3-4 minutes.
3. Stir in the chili powder, ground cumin, paprika, dried oregano, salt, and black pepper. Cook for another minute until fragrant.
4. Pour in the lime juice and chicken broth, stirring to deglaze the bottom of the pot.
5. Close the Instant Pot lid and set the valve to "Sealing." Cook on high pressure for 5 minutes.
6. Once the cooking time is complete, allow for a natural pressure release for 5 minutes, then carefully do a quick pressure release.
7. Open the Instant Pot lid and stir the chicken fajita mixture.

8. Serve the Keto Instant Pot Chicken Fajitas hot, with your choice of toppings such as shredded cheese, sour cream, guacamole, salsa, chopped cilantro, and lime wedges.
9. Optionally, serve the chicken fajita mixture in low-carb tortillas or lettuce wraps for a complete meal.

Enjoy these flavorful and satisfying Keto Instant Pot Chicken Fajitas for a delicious low-carb dinner!

**Keto Instant Pot Bacon and Cheese Egg Bites**

Ingredients:

- 6 large eggs
- 1/4 cup (60ml) heavy cream
- 1/2 cup (50g) shredded cheddar cheese
- 1/4 cup (25g) crumbled cooked bacon
- 1/4 cup (25g) chopped green onions
- Salt and black pepper, to taste
- Cooking spray or melted butter, for greasing

Instructions:

1. In a large mixing bowl, whisk together the eggs and heavy cream until well combined.
2. Stir in the shredded cheddar cheese, crumbled cooked bacon, chopped green onions, salt, and black pepper.
3. Grease the compartments of a silicone egg bite mold with cooking spray or melted butter.
4. Pour the egg mixture evenly into the compartments of the egg bite mold, filling each about 3/4 full.
5. Cover the egg bite mold tightly with aluminum foil.
6. Pour 1 cup of water into the Instant Pot insert and place the trivet inside.
7. Carefully lower the egg bite mold onto the trivet inside the Instant Pot.
8. Close the Instant Pot lid and set the valve to "Sealing." Cook on high pressure for 8 minutes.
9. Once the cooking time is complete, allow for a natural pressure release for 5 minutes, then carefully do a quick pressure release.
10. Open the Instant Pot lid and carefully remove the egg bite mold from the Instant Pot.
11. Let the egg bites cool for a few minutes before removing them from the mold.
12. Serve the Keto Instant Pot Bacon and Cheese Egg Bites warm as a delicious low-carb breakfast or snack.

Enjoy these savory and satisfying Keto Instant Pot Bacon and Cheese Egg Bites!

**Keto Instant Pot Creamy Chicken and Spinach**

Ingredients:

- 1.5 lbs (about 680g) boneless, skinless chicken breasts, cut into bite-sized pieces
- Salt and black pepper, to taste
- 2 tablespoons olive oil
- 3 cloves garlic, minced
- 1 onion, diced
- 1 bell pepper, diced
- 1 cup (240ml) chicken broth
- 1 cup (240ml) heavy cream
- 1/2 cup (50g) grated Parmesan cheese
- 2 cups (60g) fresh spinach leaves
- 1 teaspoon dried thyme
- 1 teaspoon dried rosemary
- Salt and black pepper, to taste
- Fresh parsley, chopped, for garnish

Instructions:

1. Season the chicken breast pieces with salt and black pepper.
2. Set your Instant Pot to "Saute" mode and add the olive oil. Once hot, add the seasoned chicken pieces and cook until browned on all sides, about 3-4 minutes. Remove the chicken from the Instant Pot and set aside.
3. In the same Instant Pot, add the minced garlic, diced onion, and diced bell pepper. Cook until softened, about 3-4 minutes.
4. Pour in the chicken broth and deglaze the bottom of the pot, scraping up any browned bits.
5. Return the browned chicken pieces to the Instant Pot.
6. Stir in the heavy cream, grated Parmesan cheese, fresh spinach leaves, dried thyme, and dried rosemary.
7. Close the Instant Pot lid and set the valve to "Sealing." Cook on high pressure for 5 minutes.
8. Once the cooking time is complete, allow for a natural pressure release for 5 minutes, then carefully do a quick pressure release.
9. Open the Instant Pot lid and stir the creamy chicken and spinach mixture.
10. Season with additional salt and black pepper to taste if needed.

11. Serve the Keto Instant Pot Creamy Chicken and Spinach hot, garnished with chopped fresh parsley.

Enjoy this rich and flavorful Keto Instant Pot Creamy Chicken and Spinach for a comforting low-carb meal!

**Keto Instant Pot Pork Ribs with Dry Rub**

Ingredients:

For the dry rub:

- 2 tablespoons paprika
- 1 tablespoon garlic powder
- 1 tablespoon onion powder
- 1 tablespoon ground cumin
- 1 tablespoon chili powder
- 1 tablespoon smoked paprika
- 1 tablespoon ground black pepper
- 1 tablespoon salt
- 1 teaspoon dried thyme
- 1 teaspoon dried oregano
- 1 teaspoon cayenne pepper (adjust to taste)

For the pork ribs:

- 3 lbs (about 1.4 kg) pork ribs
- 2 cups (480ml) beef or chicken broth
- 1/4 cup (60ml) apple cider vinegar
- 2 cloves garlic, minced
- 1/4 cup (60ml) low-carb barbecue sauce (optional)

Instructions:

1. In a small bowl, mix together all the ingredients for the dry rub until well combined.
2. Pat the pork ribs dry with paper towels. Rub the dry rub mixture all over the ribs, covering them thoroughly.
3. Set your Instant Pot to "Saute" mode and add a bit of olive oil. Once hot, sear the ribs on all sides until browned, about 3-4 minutes per side. You may need to do this in batches.
4. Once the ribs are browned, remove them from the Instant Pot and set aside.
5. Deglaze the Instant Pot by adding the beef or chicken broth and apple cider vinegar, scraping up any browned bits from the bottom of the pot.

6. Stir in the minced garlic.
7. Return the browned ribs to the Instant Pot, arranging them so they are standing up on their sides, with the meaty side facing outwards.
8. Close the Instant Pot lid and set the valve to "Sealing." Cook on high pressure for 25-30 minutes, depending on the thickness of the ribs.
9. Once the cooking time is complete, allow for a natural pressure release for 10 minutes, then carefully do a quick pressure release.
10. Open the Instant Pot lid and carefully remove the ribs to a serving platter.
11. Optionally, brush the ribs with low-carb barbecue sauce for extra flavor.
12. Serve the Keto Instant Pot Pork Ribs with Dry Rub hot, alongside your favorite low-carb sides.

Enjoy these tender and flavorful Keto Instant Pot Pork Ribs with Dry Rub for a satisfying low-carb meal!

**Keto Instant Pot Cheesy Cauliflower Rice**

Ingredients:

- 1 large head of cauliflower, cut into florets
- 2 tablespoons butter
- 2 cloves garlic, minced
- 1/2 cup (120ml) heavy cream
- 1 cup (100g) shredded cheddar cheese
- 1/4 cup (25g) grated Parmesan cheese
- Salt and black pepper, to taste
- Chopped parsley, for garnish (optional)

Instructions:

1. Place the cauliflower florets in the Instant Pot insert.
2. Add 1 cup of water to the Instant Pot.
3. Close the Instant Pot lid and set the valve to "Sealing." Cook on high pressure for 3 minutes.
4. Once the cooking time is complete, perform a quick pressure release.
5. Carefully remove the cauliflower from the Instant Pot and drain well.
6. Set the Instant Pot to "Saute" mode and add the butter. Once melted, add the minced garlic and sauté for about 1 minute until fragrant.
7. Return the drained cauliflower to the Instant Pot.
8. Add the heavy cream, shredded cheddar cheese, and grated Parmesan cheese to the pot. Stir well until the cheese is melted and the cauliflower is coated in the creamy sauce.
9. Season with salt and black pepper to taste.
10. Continue to cook for a few minutes on "Saute" mode, stirring occasionally, until the sauce thickens slightly.
11. Serve the Keto Instant Pot Cheesy Cauliflower Rice hot, garnished with chopped parsley if desired.

Enjoy this creamy and flavorful Keto Instant Pot Cheesy Cauliflower Rice as a delicious low-carb side dish!

**Keto Instant Pot Beef and Cabbage Soup**

Ingredients:

- 1 lb (about 450g) ground beef
- 1 tablespoon olive oil
- 1 onion, diced
- 2 cloves garlic, minced
- 4 cups (about 400g) shredded cabbage
- 2 carrots, diced
- 2 celery stalks, diced
- 1 can (14.5 oz) diced tomatoes, undrained
- 4 cups (960ml) beef broth
- 1 teaspoon dried thyme
- 1 teaspoon dried oregano
- Salt and black pepper, to taste
- Fresh parsley, chopped, for garnish (optional)

Instructions:

1. Set your Instant Pot to "Saute" mode and add the olive oil. Once hot, add the ground beef and cook until browned, breaking it apart with a spoon as it cooks.
2. Add the diced onion and minced garlic to the pot. Cook until the onion is softened, about 3-4 minutes.
3. Stir in the shredded cabbage, diced carrots, and diced celery. Cook for another 3-4 minutes until the vegetables begin to soften.
4. Add the diced tomatoes (with their juices), beef broth, dried thyme, and dried oregano to the pot. Stir well to combine.
5. Close the Instant Pot lid and set the valve to "Sealing." Cook on high pressure for 5 minutes.
6. Once the cooking time is complete, allow for a natural pressure release for 5 minutes, then carefully do a quick pressure release.
7. Open the Instant Pot lid and stir the soup. Season with salt and black pepper to taste.
8. Serve the Keto Instant Pot Beef and Cabbage Soup hot, garnished with chopped fresh parsley if desired.

Enjoy this hearty and nutritious Keto Instant Pot soup for a delicious low-carb meal!

**Keto Instant Pot Creamy Garlic Parmesan Pork Chops**

Ingredients:

- 4 bone-in pork chops (about 1 inch thick)
- Salt and black pepper, to taste
- 2 tablespoons olive oil
- 4 cloves garlic, minced
- 1 cup (240ml) chicken broth
- 1 cup (240ml) heavy cream
- 1/2 cup (50g) grated Parmesan cheese
- 1 teaspoon dried thyme
- 1 teaspoon dried rosemary
- 1 teaspoon dried oregano
- Salt and black pepper, to taste
- Chopped fresh parsley, for garnish (optional)

Instructions:

1. Season the pork chops with salt and black pepper on both sides.
2. Set your Instant Pot to "Saute" mode and add the olive oil. Once hot, add the pork chops and sear them on both sides until browned, about 3-4 minutes per side. You may need to do this in batches depending on the size of your Instant Pot.
3. Once the pork chops are browned, remove them from the Instant Pot and set aside.
4. In the same Instant Pot, add the minced garlic and cook for about 1 minute until fragrant.
5. Pour in the chicken broth and deglaze the bottom of the pot, scraping up any browned bits.
6. Stir in the heavy cream, grated Parmesan cheese, dried thyme, dried rosemary, and dried oregano.
7. Return the pork chops to the Instant Pot, nestling them into the creamy garlic Parmesan sauce.
8. Close the Instant Pot lid and set the valve to "Sealing." Cook on high pressure for 8 minutes.
9. Once the cooking time is complete, allow for a natural pressure release for 5 minutes, then carefully do a quick pressure release.

10. Open the Instant Pot lid and stir the creamy garlic Parmesan sauce.
11. Season the sauce with salt and black pepper to taste if needed.
12. Serve the Keto Instant Pot Creamy Garlic Parmesan Pork Chops hot, garnished with chopped fresh parsley if desired.

Enjoy these tender and flavorful Keto Instant Pot pork chops for a delicious low-carb meal!

**Keto Instant Pot Chicken and Bacon Chowder**

Ingredients:

- 4 slices bacon, chopped
- 1 lb (about 450g) boneless, skinless chicken thighs, diced
- Salt and black pepper, to taste
- 1 onion, diced
- 2 cloves garlic, minced
- 2 cups (about 200g) cauliflower florets
- 1 cup (240ml) chicken broth
- 1 cup (240ml) heavy cream
- 1 cup (100g) shredded cheddar cheese
- 2 tablespoons cream cheese
- 2 tablespoons chopped fresh parsley
- Optional garnishes: additional shredded cheddar cheese, chopped green onions, crispy bacon bits

Instructions:

1. Set your Instant Pot to "Saute" mode and add the chopped bacon. Cook until crispy, then remove from the pot and set aside.
2. Season the diced chicken thighs with salt and black pepper. Add them to the Instant Pot with the bacon fat and cook until browned on all sides, about 5 minutes. Remove the chicken from the pot and set aside.
3. Add the diced onion to the Instant Pot and cook until softened, about 3-4 minutes. Add the minced garlic and cook for another minute until fragrant.
4. Stir in the cauliflower florets and chicken broth. Close the Instant Pot lid and set the valve to "Sealing." Cook on high pressure for 3 minutes.
5. Once the cooking time is complete, perform a quick pressure release.
6. Open the Instant Pot lid and use an immersion blender to puree the soup until smooth. Alternatively, you can transfer the soup to a blender in batches and blend until smooth, then return it to the Instant Pot.
7. Stir in the heavy cream, shredded cheddar cheese, cream cheese, cooked chicken, and crispy bacon bits.
8. Set the Instant Pot to "Saute" mode and cook for a few more minutes until the cheese is melted and the soup is heated through.

9. Stir in the chopped fresh parsley.
10. Serve the Keto Instant Pot Chicken and Bacon Chowder hot, garnished with additional shredded cheddar cheese, chopped green onions, and crispy bacon bits if desired.

Enjoy this creamy and comforting Keto Instant Pot chicken and bacon chowder for a delicious low-carb meal!

**Keto Instant Pot Italian Sausage and Peppers**

Ingredients:

- 1 lb (about 450g) Italian sausage links (sweet or spicy), cut into chunks
- 1 tablespoon olive oil
- 1 onion, sliced
- 2 bell peppers, sliced (use a mix of colors for visual appeal)
- 3 cloves garlic, minced
- 1 can (14.5 oz) diced tomatoes, undrained
- 1 teaspoon dried oregano
- 1 teaspoon dried basil
- Salt and black pepper, to taste
- Fresh parsley, chopped, for garnish (optional)

Instructions:

1. Set your Instant Pot to "Saute" mode and add the olive oil. Once hot, add the Italian sausage chunks and cook until browned on all sides, about 5 minutes. Remove the sausage from the Instant Pot and set aside.
2. Add the sliced onion and bell peppers to the Instant Pot. Cook until softened, about 3-4 minutes.
3. Stir in the minced garlic and cook for another minute until fragrant.
4. Return the browned Italian sausage to the Instant Pot.
5. Pour in the diced tomatoes (with their juices) and add the dried oregano and dried basil. Stir well to combine.
6. Close the Instant Pot lid and set the valve to "Sealing." Cook on high pressure for 5 minutes.
7. Once the cooking time is complete, perform a quick pressure release.
8. Open the Instant Pot lid and stir the sausage and peppers mixture. Season with salt and black pepper to taste.
9. Serve the Keto Instant Pot Italian Sausage and Peppers hot, garnished with chopped fresh parsley if desired.

Enjoy this delicious and hearty Keto Instant Pot Italian Sausage and Peppers for a satisfying low-carb meal!

**Keto Instant Pot Mississippi Pot Roast**

Ingredients:

- 3-4 lbs (about 1.4-1.8 kg) beef chuck roast
- Salt and black pepper, to taste
- 2 tablespoons olive oil
- 1 packet (about 1 oz) ranch seasoning mix (check for low-carb options or make your own)
- 1 packet (about 1 oz) au jus gravy mix (check for low-carb options or make your own)
- 1/4 cup (60g) unsalted butter
- 6-8 pepperoncini peppers
- 1/4 cup (60ml) pepperoncini juice
- 1/2 cup (120ml) beef broth

Instructions:

1. Pat the beef chuck roast dry with paper towels and season generously with salt and black pepper.
2. Set your Instant Pot to "Saute" mode and add the olive oil. Once hot, add the seasoned chuck roast and sear it on all sides until browned, about 3-4 minutes per side. Remove the roast from the Instant Pot and set aside.
3. In the same Instant Pot, add the ranch seasoning mix and au jus gravy mix. Stir in the unsalted butter until melted.
4. Return the seared chuck roast to the Instant Pot, nestling it into the seasoning mixture.
5. Place the pepperoncini peppers on top of the roast and pour the pepperoncini juice and beef broth over the roast.
6. Close the Instant Pot lid and set the valve to "Sealing." Cook on high pressure for 60 minutes.
7. Once the cooking time is complete, allow for a natural pressure release for 10-15 minutes, then carefully do a quick pressure release.
8. Open the Instant Pot lid and use tongs to transfer the pot roast to a serving platter.
9. Use a spoon to skim off any excess fat from the cooking liquid in the Instant Pot.

10. Serve the Keto Instant Pot Mississippi Pot Roast hot, spooning the flavorful gravy and pepperoncini peppers over the roast slices.

Enjoy this tender and flavorful Keto Instant Pot Mississippi Pot Roast for a comforting low-carb meal!

**Keto Instant Pot Lemon Butter Salmon**

Ingredients:

- 4 salmon fillets (about 6 oz each)
- Salt and black pepper, to taste
- 2 tablespoons olive oil
- 4 cloves garlic, minced
- Zest and juice of 1 lemon
- 1/4 cup (60ml) chicken broth or white wine (for deglazing)
- 1/4 cup (60g) unsalted butter, cubed
- 1 tablespoon chopped fresh parsley
- Lemon slices, for garnish
- Fresh parsley, for garnish

Instructions:

1. Season the salmon fillets with salt and black pepper on both sides.
2. Set your Instant Pot to "Saute" mode and add the olive oil. Once hot, add the seasoned salmon fillets to the Instant Pot, skin-side down, and sear them for about 2 minutes on each side until lightly browned. Remove the salmon fillets from the Instant Pot and set aside.
3. In the same Instant Pot, add the minced garlic and cook for about 1 minute until fragrant.
4. Deglaze the Instant Pot with the chicken broth or white wine, scraping up any browned bits from the bottom of the pot.
5. Add the lemon zest and lemon juice to the Instant Pot, stirring to combine.
6. Return the seared salmon fillets to the Instant Pot, arranging them in a single layer.
7. Place the cubed unsalted butter on top of the salmon fillets.
8. Close the Instant Pot lid and set the valve to "Sealing." Cook on high pressure for 3 minutes.
9. Once the cooking time is complete, allow for a natural pressure release for 5 minutes, then carefully do a quick pressure release.
10. Open the Instant Pot lid and carefully remove the salmon fillets to a serving platter.

11. Stir the sauce in the Instant Pot until well combined. Taste and adjust seasoning if needed.
12. Spoon the lemon butter sauce over the salmon fillets.
13. Garnish with chopped fresh parsley and lemon slices.
14. Serve the Keto Instant Pot Lemon Butter Salmon hot, accompanied by your favorite side dishes.

Enjoy this flavorful and tender Keto Instant Pot Lemon Butter Salmon for a delicious low-carb meal!

**Keto Instant Pot Beef Stroganoff**

Ingredients:

- 1.5 lbs (about 680g) beef sirloin steak, thinly sliced
- Salt and black pepper, to taste
- 2 tablespoons olive oil
- 1 onion, diced
- 3 cloves garlic, minced
- 8 oz (about 225g) mushrooms, sliced
- 1 tablespoon tomato paste
- 1 cup (240ml) beef broth
- 1 tablespoon Worcestershire sauce
- 1 teaspoon Dijon mustard
- 1 cup (240ml) heavy cream
- 2 tablespoons cream cheese
- 2 tablespoons sour cream
- 2 tablespoons chopped fresh parsley, for garnish (optional)
- Cauliflower rice or zucchini noodles, for serving (optional)

Instructions:

1. Season the thinly sliced beef sirloin steak with salt and black pepper.
2. Set your Instant Pot to "Saute" mode and add the olive oil. Once hot, add the seasoned beef slices and sear them in batches until browned on all sides, about 2-3 minutes per batch. Remove the beef from the Instant Pot and set aside.
3. In the same Instant Pot, add the diced onion and cook until softened, about 3-4 minutes.
4. Add the minced garlic and sliced mushrooms to the Instant Pot. Cook until the mushrooms are softened and browned, about 5 minutes.
5. Stir in the tomato paste and cook for another minute.
6. Pour in the beef broth, Worcestershire sauce, and Dijon mustard, scraping up any browned bits from the bottom of the pot.
7. Return the seared beef slices to the Instant Pot, along with any accumulated juices.
8. Close the Instant Pot lid and set the valve to "Sealing." Cook on high pressure for 10 minutes.

9. Once the cooking time is complete, allow for a natural pressure release for 10 minutes, then carefully do a quick pressure release.
10. Open the Instant Pot lid and set it to "Saute" mode. Stir in the heavy cream, cream cheese, and sour cream until well combined.
11. Let the mixture simmer for a few minutes until the sauce has thickened slightly.
12. Taste and adjust seasoning with salt and black pepper if needed.
13. Serve the Keto Instant Pot Beef Stroganoff hot, garnished with chopped fresh parsley if desired, and accompanied by cauliflower rice or zucchini noodles if desired.

Enjoy this creamy and flavorful Keto Instant Pot Beef Stroganoff for a satisfying low-carb meal!

**Keto Instant Pot Creamy Garlic Parmesan Chicken**

Ingredients:

- 4 boneless, skinless chicken breasts
- Salt and black pepper, to taste
- 2 tablespoons olive oil
- 4 cloves garlic, minced
- 1 cup (240ml) chicken broth
- 1 cup (240ml) heavy cream
- 1/2 cup (50g) grated Parmesan cheese
- 1 teaspoon dried thyme
- 1 teaspoon dried rosemary
- 1 teaspoon dried oregano
- Salt and black pepper, to taste
- Fresh parsley, chopped, for garnish (optional)

Instructions:

1. Season the chicken breasts with salt and black pepper on both sides.
2. Set your Instant Pot to "Saute" mode and add the olive oil. Once hot, add the seasoned chicken breasts and sear them on both sides until golden brown, about 3-4 minutes per side. Remove the chicken breasts from the Instant Pot and set aside.
3. In the same Instant Pot, add the minced garlic and cook for about 1 minute until fragrant.
4. Pour in the chicken broth and deglaze the bottom of the pot, scraping up any browned bits.
5. Stir in the heavy cream, grated Parmesan cheese, dried thyme, dried rosemary, and dried oregano until well combined.
6. Return the seared chicken breasts to the Instant Pot, nestling them into the creamy garlic Parmesan sauce.
7. Close the Instant Pot lid and set the valve to "Sealing." Cook on high pressure for 8 minutes.
8. Once the cooking time is complete, allow for a natural pressure release for 5 minutes, then carefully do a quick pressure release.

9. Open the Instant Pot lid and stir the creamy garlic Parmesan sauce. Taste and adjust seasoning with salt and black pepper if needed.
10. Serve the Keto Instant Pot Creamy Garlic Parmesan Chicken hot, garnished with chopped fresh parsley if desired.

Enjoy this rich and flavorful Keto Instant Pot Creamy Garlic Parmesan Chicken for a delicious low-carb meal!

# Keto Instant Pot Broccoli Cheese Soup

Ingredients:

- 4 cups (about 400g) broccoli florets
- 4 cups (960ml) chicken or vegetable broth
- 1 small onion, chopped
- 2 cloves garlic, minced
- 1/4 cup (60g) unsalted butter
- 1/4 cup (30g) almond flour
- 1 cup (240ml) heavy cream
- 2 cups (200g) shredded cheddar cheese
- Salt and black pepper, to taste
- Optional toppings: additional shredded cheddar cheese, cooked bacon bits, chopped green onions

Instructions:

1. Add the broccoli florets, chicken or vegetable broth, chopped onion, and minced garlic to the Instant Pot.
2. Close the Instant Pot lid and set the valve to "Sealing." Cook on high pressure for 5 minutes.
3. Once the cooking time is complete, perform a quick pressure release.
4. Open the Instant Pot lid and use an immersion blender to blend the soup until smooth. Alternatively, transfer the soup to a blender in batches and blend until smooth, then return it to the Instant Pot.
5. Set the Instant Pot to "Saute" mode and add the unsalted butter to melt.
6. Once the butter is melted, whisk in the almond flour until smooth, creating a roux.
7. Slowly pour in the heavy cream, whisking continuously until well combined and the soup begins to thicken.
8. Stir in the shredded cheddar cheese until melted and the soup is smooth and creamy.
9. Season the soup with salt and black pepper to taste.
10. Serve the Keto Instant Pot Broccoli Cheese Soup hot, garnished with additional shredded cheddar cheese, cooked bacon bits, and chopped green onions if desired.

Enjoy this comforting and creamy Keto Instant Pot Broccoli Cheese Soup for a satisfying low-carb meal!

**Keto Instant Pot Buffalo Chicken Dip**

Ingredients:

- 2 cups (about 240g) shredded cooked chicken
- 8 oz (about 225g) cream cheese, softened
- 1/2 cup (120ml) hot sauce (adjust to taste)
- 1/4 cup (60ml) ranch dressing
- 1/4 cup (60ml) sour cream
- 1 cup (100g) shredded cheddar cheese
- 1/4 cup (30g) crumbled blue cheese (optional)
- 2 cloves garlic, minced
- 1 teaspoon onion powder
- 1 teaspoon dried parsley
- Salt and black pepper, to taste
- Chopped green onions, for garnish (optional)
- Celery sticks, cucumber slices, or low-carb crackers, for serving

Instructions:

1. In the Instant Pot, combine the shredded chicken, softened cream cheese, hot sauce, ranch dressing, sour cream, shredded cheddar cheese, crumbled blue cheese (if using), minced garlic, onion powder, dried parsley, salt, and black pepper. Stir until well combined.
2. Close the Instant Pot lid and set the valve to "Sealing." Cook on high pressure for 5 minutes.
3. Once the cooking time is complete, perform a quick pressure release.
4. Open the Instant Pot lid and give the Buffalo chicken dip a good stir.
5. If desired, switch the Instant Pot to "Saute" mode and cook the dip for a few more minutes to thicken it up slightly, stirring frequently.
6. Serve the Keto Instant Pot Buffalo Chicken Dip hot, garnished with chopped green onions if desired. Serve with celery sticks, cucumber slices, or low-carb crackers for dipping.

Enjoy this creamy and spicy Keto Instant Pot Buffalo Chicken Dip as a delicious appetizer or snack!

## Keto Instant Pot Mexican Shredded Chicken

Ingredients:

- 2 lbs (about 900g) boneless, skinless chicken breasts or thighs
- 1 onion, diced
- 2 cloves garlic, minced
- 1 can (10 oz) diced tomatoes with green chilies, drained
- 1 tablespoon chili powder
- 1 teaspoon ground cumin
- 1 teaspoon smoked paprika
- 1/2 teaspoon dried oregano
- 1/2 teaspoon onion powder
- 1/2 teaspoon garlic powder
- 1/2 teaspoon salt
- 1/4 teaspoon black pepper
- 1/4 cup (60ml) chicken broth or water
- Juice of 1 lime
- Chopped fresh cilantro, for garnish (optional)

Instructions:

1. In the Instant Pot, combine the diced onion, minced garlic, drained diced tomatoes with green chilies, chili powder, ground cumin, smoked paprika, dried oregano, onion powder, garlic powder, salt, black pepper, and chicken broth or water. Stir until well combined.
2. Add the boneless, skinless chicken breasts or thighs to the Instant Pot, nestling them into the sauce.
3. Close the Instant Pot lid and set the valve to "Sealing." Cook on high pressure for 12 minutes for chicken breasts or 15 minutes for chicken thighs.
4. Once the cooking time is complete, allow for a natural pressure release for 10 minutes, then carefully do a quick pressure release.
5. Open the Instant Pot lid and use two forks to shred the chicken in the pot.
6. Stir in the lime juice and chopped fresh cilantro if desired.
7. Serve the Keto Instant Pot Mexican Shredded Chicken hot, as a filling for tacos, burritos, lettuce wraps, salads, or bowls.

Enjoy this flavorful and versatile Keto Instant Pot Mexican Shredded Chicken in your favorite Mexican-inspired dishes!

**Keto Instant Pot Beef Brisket**

Ingredients:

- 3-4 lbs (about 1.4-1.8 kg) beef brisket
- Salt and black pepper, to taste
- 2 tablespoons olive oil
- 1 onion, sliced
- 4 cloves garlic, minced
- 1 cup (240ml) beef broth
- 1/4 cup (60ml) apple cider vinegar
- 2 tablespoons Worcestershire sauce
- 1 tablespoon Dijon mustard
- 1 tablespoon paprika
- 1 teaspoon dried thyme
- 1 teaspoon dried rosemary
- 1 teaspoon garlic powder
- 1 teaspoon onion powder
- 1/2 teaspoon cayenne pepper (optional, for heat)
- Chopped fresh parsley, for garnish (optional)

Instructions:

1. Season the beef brisket generously with salt and black pepper on both sides.
2. Set your Instant Pot to "Saute" mode and add the olive oil. Once hot, add the seasoned beef brisket and sear it on both sides until browned, about 3-4 minutes per side. Remove the brisket from the Instant Pot and set aside.
3. In the same Instant Pot, add the sliced onion and minced garlic. Cook until softened, about 3-4 minutes.
4. Stir in the beef broth, apple cider vinegar, Worcestershire sauce, Dijon mustard, paprika, dried thyme, dried rosemary, garlic powder, onion powder, and cayenne pepper (if using). Mix well to combine.
5. Return the seared beef brisket to the Instant Pot, nestling it into the liquid and onions.
6. Close the Instant Pot lid and set the valve to "Sealing." Cook on high pressure for 60-70 minutes, depending on the size and thickness of the brisket.

7. Once the cooking time is complete, allow for a natural pressure release for 10-15 minutes, then carefully do a quick pressure release.
8. Open the Instant Pot lid and carefully transfer the beef brisket to a cutting board.
9. Let the brisket rest for a few minutes, then slice it against the grain into thin slices.
10. Serve the Keto Instant Pot Beef Brisket hot, garnished with chopped fresh parsley if desired.

Enjoy this tender and flavorful Keto Instant Pot Beef Brisket as a hearty and satisfying meal!

**Keto Instant Pot Creamy Tuscan Pork Chops**

Ingredients:

- 4 boneless pork chops
- Salt and black pepper, to taste
- 2 tablespoons olive oil
- 4 cloves garlic, minced
- 1/2 cup (120ml) chicken broth
- 1 cup (240ml) heavy cream
- 1/4 cup (25g) grated Parmesan cheese
- 1/4 cup (60g) sun-dried tomatoes, chopped
- 1/4 cup (30g) chopped spinach (fresh or frozen)
- 1 teaspoon dried basil
- 1 teaspoon dried oregano
- 1/2 teaspoon dried thyme
- 1/4 teaspoon red pepper flakes (optional, for heat)
- Salt and black pepper, to taste
- Chopped fresh parsley, for garnish (optional)

Instructions:

1. Season the pork chops with salt and black pepper on both sides.
2. Set your Instant Pot to "Saute" mode and add the olive oil. Once hot, add the seasoned pork chops and sear them on both sides until browned, about 3-4 minutes per side. Remove the pork chops from the Instant Pot and set aside.
3. In the same Instant Pot, add the minced garlic and cook for about 1 minute until fragrant.
4. Pour in the chicken broth and deglaze the bottom of the pot, scraping up any browned bits.
5. Stir in the heavy cream, grated Parmesan cheese, chopped sun-dried tomatoes, chopped spinach, dried basil, dried oregano, dried thyme, and red pepper flakes (if using). Mix well to combine.
6. Return the seared pork chops to the Instant Pot, nestling them into the creamy Tuscan sauce.
7. Close the Instant Pot lid and set the valve to "Sealing." Cook on high pressure for 8 minutes.

8. Once the cooking time is complete, allow for a natural pressure release for 5 minutes, then carefully do a quick pressure release.
9. Open the Instant Pot lid and stir the creamy Tuscan sauce. Taste and adjust seasoning with salt and black pepper if needed.
10. Serve the Keto Instant Pot Creamy Tuscan Pork Chops hot, garnished with chopped fresh parsley if desired.

Enjoy these tender and flavorful Keto Instant Pot Creamy Tuscan Pork Chops for a delicious low-carb meal!

**Keto Instant Pot Chicken Marsala**

Ingredients:

- 4 boneless, skinless chicken breasts
- Salt and black pepper, to taste
- 2 tablespoons olive oil
- 8 oz (about 225g) mushrooms, sliced
- 4 cloves garlic, minced
- 1 cup (240ml) chicken broth
- 1 cup (240ml) dry Marsala wine
- 1/2 cup (120ml) heavy cream
- 2 tablespoons unsalted butter
- 1 tablespoon almond flour (optional, for thickening)
- Chopped fresh parsley, for garnish (optional)

Instructions:

1. Season the chicken breasts with salt and black pepper on both sides.
2. Set your Instant Pot to "Saute" mode and add the olive oil. Once hot, add the seasoned chicken breasts and sear them on both sides until browned, about 3-4 minutes per side. Remove the chicken breasts from the Instant Pot and set aside.
3. In the same Instant Pot, add the sliced mushrooms and cook until they release their juices and start to brown, about 5 minutes.
4. Stir in the minced garlic and cook for another minute until fragrant.
5. Pour in the chicken broth and dry Marsala wine, scraping up any browned bits from the bottom of the pot.
6. Return the seared chicken breasts to the Instant Pot, nestling them into the mushroom mixture.
7. Close the Instant Pot lid and set the valve to "Sealing." Cook on high pressure for 8 minutes.
8. Once the cooking time is complete, allow for a natural pressure release for 5 minutes, then carefully do a quick pressure release.
9. Open the Instant Pot lid and remove the chicken breasts to a serving platter.
10. Set the Instant Pot to "Saute" mode and stir in the heavy cream and unsalted butter. If you prefer a thicker sauce, you can whisk in almond flour at this point.
11. Let the sauce simmer for a few minutes until it thickens slightly.
12. Taste the sauce and adjust seasoning with salt and black pepper if needed.

13. Serve the Keto Instant Pot Chicken Marsala hot, spooning the creamy mushroom Marsala sauce over the chicken breasts.
14. Garnish with chopped fresh parsley if desired.

Enjoy this rich and flavorful Keto Instant Pot Chicken Marsala for a delicious low-carb meal!

**Keto Instant Pot Ratatouille**

Ingredients:

- 1 eggplant, diced
- 2 zucchini, diced
- 2 yellow squash, diced
- 1 onion, diced
- 2 bell peppers (red, yellow, or orange), diced
- 3 cloves garlic, minced
- 1 can (14 oz) diced tomatoes, undrained
- 2 tablespoons tomato paste
- 1 teaspoon dried thyme
- 1 teaspoon dried oregano
- 1 teaspoon dried basil
- Salt and black pepper, to taste
- 2 tablespoons olive oil
- Chopped fresh parsley, for garnish (optional)

Instructions:

1. In the Instant Pot, combine the diced eggplant, zucchini, yellow squash, onion, bell peppers, minced garlic, diced tomatoes, tomato paste, dried thyme, dried oregano, dried basil, salt, and black pepper. Stir until well combined.
2. Drizzle the olive oil over the top of the vegetable mixture.
3. Close the Instant Pot lid and set the valve to "Sealing." Cook on high pressure for 5 minutes.
4. Once the cooking time is complete, allow for a natural pressure release for 5 minutes, then carefully do a quick pressure release.
5. Open the Instant Pot lid and give the ratatouille a good stir.
6. Taste and adjust seasoning with salt and black pepper if needed.
7. Serve the Keto Instant Pot Ratatouille hot, garnished with chopped fresh parsley if desired.

Enjoy this flavorful and vibrant Keto Instant Pot Ratatouille as a delicious side dish or vegetarian main course!

# Keto Instant Pot Coconut Lime Chicken

Ingredients:

- 4 boneless, skinless chicken breasts
- Salt and black pepper, to taste
- 2 tablespoons olive oil
- 1 onion, finely chopped
- 3 cloves garlic, minced
- 1 tablespoon ginger, minced
- 1 can (13.5 oz) coconut milk
- Zest and juice of 2 limes
- 2 tablespoons soy sauce or tamari (for gluten-free)
- 1 tablespoon fish sauce
- 1 tablespoon erythritol or low-carb sweetener of choice
- 1 teaspoon chili flakes (optional, for heat)
- Chopped fresh cilantro, for garnish (optional)
- Lime wedges, for serving

Instructions:

1. Season the chicken breasts with salt and black pepper on both sides.
2. Set your Instant Pot to "Saute" mode and add the olive oil. Once hot, add the seasoned chicken breasts and sear them on both sides until browned, about 3-4 minutes per side. Remove the chicken breasts from the Instant Pot and set aside.
3. In the same Instant Pot, add the chopped onion and cook until softened, about 3-4 minutes.
4. Stir in the minced garlic and ginger, and cook for another minute until fragrant.
5. Pour in the coconut milk, lime zest, lime juice, soy sauce or tamari, fish sauce, erythritol or low-carb sweetener, and chili flakes (if using). Mix well to combine.
6. Return the seared chicken breasts to the Instant Pot, nestling them into the coconut lime sauce.
7. Close the Instant Pot lid and set the valve to "Sealing." Cook on high pressure for 8 minutes.
8. Once the cooking time is complete, allow for a natural pressure release for 5 minutes, then carefully do a quick pressure release.
9. Open the Instant Pot lid and remove the chicken breasts to a serving platter.

10. Set the Instant Pot to "Saute" mode and let the sauce simmer for a few minutes to thicken slightly.
11. Taste the sauce and adjust seasoning with salt and black pepper if needed.
12. Serve the Keto Instant Pot Coconut Lime Chicken hot, garnished with chopped fresh cilantro if desired, and lime wedges on the side.

Enjoy this fragrant and flavorful Keto Instant Pot Coconut Lime Chicken for a delicious low-carb meal!

## Keto Instant Pot Beef Bone Broth

Ingredients:

- 2-3 lbs (about 900g - 1.4kg) beef bones (such as marrow bones, knuckle bones, or a combination)
- 2 carrots, roughly chopped
- 2 celery stalks, roughly chopped
- 1 onion, quartered
- 4 cloves garlic, smashed
- 2 bay leaves
- 1 tablespoon apple cider vinegar
- Water, enough to cover the bones
- Salt and black pepper, to taste (optional)

Instructions:

1. Preheat your oven to 400°F (200°C). Place the beef bones on a baking sheet and roast them in the oven for about 30 minutes, or until they are well browned.
2. Transfer the roasted beef bones to your Instant Pot. Add the chopped carrots, celery, onion, smashed garlic cloves, bay leaves, and apple cider vinegar.
3. Fill the Instant Pot with enough water to cover the bones, but do not exceed the maximum fill line.
4. Close the Instant Pot lid and set the valve to "Sealing." Cook on high pressure for 120 minutes (2 hours).
5. Once the cooking time is complete, allow for a natural pressure release. This may take some time due to the volume of liquid.
6. Once the pressure has released and it's safe to open the Instant Pot, carefully remove the lid.
7. Use a fine mesh strainer or cheesecloth to strain the broth, removing any solids. Discard the solids.
8. Let the broth cool slightly before transferring it to storage containers. You can refrigerate the broth for up to 5 days or freeze it for longer storage.
9. Before serving, you can season the broth with salt and black pepper to taste, if desired.

Enjoy this rich and flavorful Keto Instant Pot Beef Bone Broth as a nourishing base for soups, stews, or sipped on its own for a comforting warm drink.

**Keto Instant Pot Cauliflower Soup**

Ingredients:

- 1 head cauliflower, chopped into florets
- 1 onion, diced
- 2 cloves garlic, minced
- 2 cups (480ml) chicken or vegetable broth
- 1 cup (240ml) heavy cream
- 1/2 cup (120ml) water
- 1/4 cup (60g) cream cheese
- 1/4 cup (30g) grated Parmesan cheese
- 2 tablespoons unsalted butter
- Salt and black pepper, to taste
- Optional toppings: crispy bacon bits, chopped chives, shredded cheddar cheese

Instructions:

1. Set your Instant Pot to "Saute" mode and melt the unsalted butter. Add the diced onion and minced garlic, and cook until softened, about 3-4 minutes.
2. Add the chopped cauliflower florets to the Instant Pot, along with the chicken or vegetable broth and water.
3. Close the Instant Pot lid and set the valve to "Sealing." Cook on high pressure for 5 minutes.
4. Once the cooking time is complete, allow for a natural pressure release for 5 minutes, then carefully do a quick pressure release.
5. Open the Instant Pot lid and use an immersion blender to puree the soup until smooth. Alternatively, you can transfer the soup to a blender in batches and blend until smooth, then return it to the Instant Pot.
6. Set the Instant Pot to "Saute" mode again and stir in the heavy cream, cream cheese, and grated Parmesan cheese until well combined. Let the soup simmer for a few minutes until heated through and slightly thickened.
7. Taste the soup and adjust seasoning with salt and black pepper as needed.
8. Serve the Keto Instant Pot Cauliflower Soup hot, garnished with optional toppings like crispy bacon bits, chopped chives, or shredded cheddar cheese.

Enjoy this creamy and satisfying Keto Instant Pot Cauliflower Soup for a comforting low-carb meal!

**Keto Instant Pot Lemon Herb Chicken**

Ingredients:

- 4 boneless, skinless chicken breasts
- Salt and black pepper, to taste
- 2 tablespoons olive oil
- 4 cloves garlic, minced
- Zest and juice of 2 lemons
- 1 cup (240ml) chicken broth
- 1 tablespoon dried thyme
- 1 tablespoon dried rosemary
- 1 tablespoon dried oregano
- 1 teaspoon dried basil
- 1/2 teaspoon red pepper flakes (optional, for heat)
- Chopped fresh parsley, for garnish (optional)

Instructions:

1. Season the chicken breasts with salt and black pepper on both sides.
2. Set your Instant Pot to "Saute" mode and add the olive oil. Once hot, add the seasoned chicken breasts and sear them on both sides until browned, about 3-4 minutes per side. Remove the chicken breasts from the Instant Pot and set aside.
3. In the same Instant Pot, add the minced garlic and cook for about 1 minute until fragrant.
4. Pour in the chicken broth and deglaze the bottom of the pot, scraping up any browned bits.
5. Stir in the lemon zest, lemon juice, dried thyme, dried rosemary, dried oregano, dried basil, and red pepper flakes (if using). Mix well to combine.
6. Return the seared chicken breasts to the Instant Pot, nestling them into the lemon herb sauce.
7. Close the Instant Pot lid and set the valve to "Sealing." Cook on high pressure for 8 minutes.
8. Once the cooking time is complete, allow for a natural pressure release for 5 minutes, then carefully do a quick pressure release.
9. Open the Instant Pot lid and remove the chicken breasts to a serving platter.
10. Set the Instant Pot to "Saute" mode and let the sauce simmer for a few minutes to thicken slightly.

11. Taste the sauce and adjust seasoning with salt and black pepper if needed.
12. Serve the Keto Instant Pot Lemon Herb Chicken hot, garnished with chopped fresh parsley if desired.

Enjoy this bright and flavorful Keto Instant Pot Lemon Herb Chicken for a delicious low-carb meal!

## Keto Instant Pot Green Chile Pork Stew

Ingredients:

- 2 lbs (about 900g) pork shoulder or pork butt, cut into bite-sized cubes
- Salt and black pepper, to taste
- 2 tablespoons olive oil
- 1 onion, diced
- 4 cloves garlic, minced
- 2 cans (4 oz each) diced green chilies
- 2 cups (480ml) chicken broth
- 1 teaspoon ground cumin
- 1 teaspoon dried oregano
- 1/2 teaspoon ground coriander
- 1/4 teaspoon cayenne pepper (optional, for heat)
- 1/4 cup (60ml) heavy cream
- Chopped fresh cilantro, for garnish (optional)
- Lime wedges, for serving

Instructions:

1. Season the pork cubes with salt and black pepper.
2. Set your Instant Pot to "Saute" mode and add the olive oil. Once hot, add the seasoned pork cubes and sear them on all sides until browned, about 5 minutes. Remove the pork from the Instant Pot and set aside.
3. In the same Instant Pot, add the diced onion and cook until softened, about 3-4 minutes.
4. Stir in the minced garlic and cook for another minute until fragrant.
5. Add the diced green chilies (with their juices) to the Instant Pot, along with the chicken broth, ground cumin, dried oregano, ground coriander, and cayenne pepper (if using). Mix well to combine.
6. Return the seared pork cubes to the Instant Pot, nestling them into the green chili mixture.
7. Close the Instant Pot lid and set the valve to "Sealing." Cook on high pressure for 30 minutes.
8. Once the cooking time is complete, allow for a natural pressure release for 10 minutes, then carefully do a quick pressure release.

9. Open the Instant Pot lid and stir in the heavy cream.
10. Taste the stew and adjust seasoning with salt and black pepper if needed.
11. Serve the Keto Instant Pot Green Chile Pork Stew hot, garnished with chopped fresh cilantro if desired, and lime wedges on the side.

Enjoy this flavorful and comforting Keto Instant Pot Green Chile Pork Stew for a satisfying low-carb meal!

www.ingramcontent.com/pod-product-compliance
Lightning Source LLC
LaVergne TN
LVHW081610060526
838201LV00054B/2180